W9-BBB-635

EARTH

KEEPERS

Written by Stuart A. Kallen

Published by Abdo & Daughters, 4940 Viking Drive, Suite 622, Edina, Minnesota 55435.

Library bound edition distributed by Rockbottom Books, Pentagon Tower, P.O. Box 36036, Minneapolis, Minnesota 55435.

Edited by John Shepard

LIBRARY OF CONGRESS CATALOGING-IN-PUBLICATION DATA

Kallen, Stuart A., 1955 -
  Earth keepers/ written by Stuart A. Kallen.
    p.   cm. -- (Target earth)
  Includes bibliographical references and index.
  Summary: Examines the lives of three people who were pioneer naturalists and ecologists.
  ISBN 1-56239-211-5
    1. Carson, Rachel. 1907-1964 -- Juvenile literature. 2. Muir, John, 1838-1914 -- Juvenile literature. 3. Cousteau, Jacques Yves -- Juvenile literature. 4. Ecologists -- United States -- Biography -- Juvenile literature. 5. Environmentalists -- United States -- Biography -- Juvenile literature. 6. Naturalists -- United States -- Biography -- Juvenile literature. 7. Conservationists -- United States -- Biography -- Juvenile literature. 8. Oceanographers -- France -- Biography -- Juvenile literature. [1. Carson, Rachel, 1907-1964. 2. Muir, John, 1838-1914. 3. Cousteau, Jacques Yves, 4. Ecologists. 5. Environmentalists.] I. Title.   II. Series.
    QH26.C27K34 1993
    333.7'2'0922--dc20
    [B]   93-15329
                                                                   CIP
                                   T 51778   333.7 AC
                                                          KAL

 Thanks To The Trees From Which This Recycled Paper Was First Made.

Table of Contents

Let's Begin Here.

VOICES IN THE WILDERNESS

In centuries gone by, those who dedicated their lives to learning about nature were called naturalists. A naturalist today might study zoology (animal life), botany (plant life), or ecology (how plants and animals relate to the world around them).

Untouched wilderness areas are being destroyed by pollution and human population growth. As this happens, people are taking more of an interest in nature and the workings of the natural world. Today such people are called environmentalists. As luck would have it (for ourselves and the Earth), their numbers are growing every day.

The people whose lives are detailed in this book were pioneer naturalists and ecologists. They raised their voices to save Earth at a time when few thought twice about clear-cutting a forest or spraying pesticides on a wetland. Some of the last wilderness areas left in the world are preserved today because of the the work of these Earth keepers. They had the vision to motivate governments and to inspire citizens to save some wilderness for the future.

John Muir is responsible for saving millions of acres of wilderness. He has several parks named after him including Muir Woods in California.

Rachel Carson pointed out the extreme dangers of some pesticides. She did it during a period in history when those chemicals were carelessly sprayed everywhere. Carson put her career and reputation on the line to protect the delicate web of life.

Jacques Cousteau, with his wife and friends, invented scuba diving gear. They used the diving equipment to explore and make movies under water. Cousteau can take credit for helping save and protect vast stretches of the mysterious world beneath the sea. Cousteau has also educated people and helped protect rivers and fresh-water lakes.

Once the Earth keepers were just a few lonely voices in the wilderness. But they inspired a worldwide environmental movement that you can be part of. When you read the stories of the Earth keepers you can see that one person can make a difference. A group of people united can stop pollution, can stop wasteful timber cutting, and can stop animal extinction. You, too, can make a difference for your children and your children's children's children.

JOHN MUIR
A ride on snow stars

A fresh snow had just fallen in California's Yosemite (pronounced "yo-SEM-i-tee") Valley. Huge cliffs rose from the valley floor and the towering granite peaks were robed in a dazzling white blanket of drifts. The year was 1885.

A lone figure stood in the valley gazing at his goal thousands of feet above him. The mountain man squinted into a sky that was as blue as his eyes. He thoughtfully stroked his long, tangled, reddish-brown beard. Without delay he set out for the summit of Yosemite Point, 6,936 feet (2,115 meters) above sea level. A lesser person might have snuggled into his or her sleeping bag and waited for a thaw. But this was John Muir—father of Yosemite, savior of the Sequoia trees, writer, explorer, and pioneer ecologist.

Mile after mile, Muir trudged through the waist-deep snow. At times, he was imprisoned in snow drifts as high as his chest. But with the strength of a mountain goat, he climbed to his goal. "I am always glad to touch the living rock again and dip my head in high mountain sky," Muir said.

An hour before sunset, he was only several hundred feet below Yosemite Point. From that high place, Muir could gaze at the Sierra Nevada Mountains as few people had ever done. His day had been filled with some of the most breathtaking wilderness scenery on Earth. He could see granite peaks rolling away for dozens of miles in each direction.

Suddenly from above, Muir heard the dull rumble that strikes terror into the hearts of all mountain climbers. Avalanche! Millions of gently layered snowflakes suddenly snowballed into a destructive force of nature. In an instant, Muir was hurtling towards the valley on a smashing, crashing surge of snow.

John Muir

John Muir (1838-1914), American naturalist,
instrumental in establishing Yosemite National Park.

The Sierra Mountains in northern California,
where John Muir spent much of his time.

As luck would have it, Muir was not buried alive under the tons of snow. At the last minute he spread his arms and legs and threw himself on top of the avalanche. This spread-eagle position allowed him to ride the crest of the snow wave. With his long hair and beard blowing straight out behind him, Muir cackled with laughter as he took his free ride down the mountain. Within minutes he was back on the valley floor, as he later wrote, "on top of the crumpled pile of snow without a bruise or scar."

Such a near-death experience would have made most people give up mountain climbing forever. But not John Muir. He was in ecstasy. He wrote in his journal, "Elijah's flight in a chariot of fire could hardly have been more gloriously exciting." Muir had loved his ride on what he called "a Milky Way of snow-stars."

If John Muir had not lived, the United States would look far different than it does today. Muir explored many nooks and crannies of American wilderness, usually alone. He rambled thousands of miles across the country, from the swamps of Florida to the barren glaciers of Alaska. He lobbied to save the Grand Canyon, Washington's Olympic Peninsula, Yosemite Valley, and more. He discovered plants and insects. Today schools, lakes, mountains, and trails are named after him. In California, more places are named after John Muir than any other person.

Muir was as rugged as the lands he traveled. He once said that to prepare for a trip he would "throw some tea and bread in a sack and jump over the backyard fence." Late in life his writings made him rich and famous. But when asked to define his job, he answered, "Tramp! I'm seventy-four and still good at it."

From Scotland to the "University of Wilderness"

John Muir started life in the village of Dunbar, carved into the cliffs of Scotland on the North Sea. Born April 12, 1838, he grew up as the oldest of eight children. Muir's father was a strict, stern man who beat him for even the most minor offenses. By the time he was five years old, Muir often ran away from his father. He went down to the sea and listened to the birds sing and the waves crash upon the beach.

In February 1849, Muir's family moved to America. They spent two months at sea before arriving in New York City. A river boat took them to Albany and down the Erie Canal to Buffalo. Then on another boat they crossed the Great Lakes to Milwaukee. There they loaded their belongings in a horse-drawn wagon and pushed deep into the Wisconsin wilderness.

The Muirs settled on eighty acres of land near the Fox River. After clearing the land, they worked sunrise to sunset growing corn and wheat. In the hard Wisconsin winters the family of ten huddled around a tiny kitchen stove for warmth. When morning came, their empty shoes and socks were sometimes frozen solid.

Muir's father worked his family endlessly. They took only two days off each year—the Fourth of July and New Year's Day. Once John's father forced him to dig a well. The young man cut and scraped the earth using nothing but a hammer and chisel until he finally struck water 90 feet (27.9 meters) below the surface.

Young John wanted more from life. At night while his family slept, he arose and tinkered in his workshop, building saws, compasses, clocks, and several inventions. He whittled gears and gizmos out of wood. He even invented an "early-rising" machine. When the alarm went off, a rod would tip his bed upright and the sleepy Muir would find himself standing.

But John's stern father thought his inventions were, in Muir's words, "of little importance."

Muir left the farm in 1860 to show his inventions at the Wisconsin State Fair in Madison. His early-rising machine won him a ten dollar prize. The inventor convinced the dean of the University of Wisconsin to let him attend the school. To make money, Muir toiled in farm fields during the summer and taught school in winter. His professors were amazed by his inventions, which included a "studying desk" that would pluck a book off a rack, open it up to a selected page for a number of minutes, then close the book and replace it with another.

But university life was not for Muir. After a few years he left the University of Wisconsin for the "University of Wilderness," as he called it. Some said Muir fled to Canada to avoid being drafted into the Civil War. Muir claimed to oppose all wars, and still considered himself a Scotsman. (He didn't become an American citizen until he was 65.) In Canada Muir wandered alone, studying plants and animals. On the advice of Jeanne Carr, the wife of one of his professors, he started writing down his thoughts and observations on nature.

After the Civil War, Muir, now 29, returned to America and took a job in a saw mill. One day tragedy struck. While working on a machine, a piece of jagged metal flew into his right eye. He stood in horror as his right eye, and then his left eye went blind.

While lying in darkness for a month, he decided he would devote himself to nature. His doctor said he would never see again. But after thirty days spent in a darkened room, thinking and praying, sight returned to John Muir's eyes.

The Thousand-mile Walk

In 1867, Muir set off for a thousand-mile walk to the Gulf of Mexico. When asked by friends where he was going, he said, "I don't know—just anywhere in the wilderness." In his journal he wrote, "I doubt if civilization will ever see me again."

Muir tramped off to the south, through Indiana and Kentucky "without speaking a word to anyone." He camped beneath "one great bedroom of the night" without a lantern, tent, compass, knife, or sleeping bag. When it rained he stood on top of the highest hill, watching lightning bolts blaze around him. When the wind blew, he climbed to the top of the tallest pine tree and for hours rode the swaying branches. Everywhere he went he kept his nature journal.

In two months Muir hiked across Kentucky, Tennessee, Georgia, and Florida. Along the way he found awe-inspiring wilderness. He also found a countryside ravaged by the Civil War. Farms had been stripped and burned and cities had been destroyed. Men who had lost everything wandered the roads, robbing and killing any who crossed their paths. Once Muir was robbed by a highway bandit. But when the thief discovered that Muir's pack contained nothing but a change of clothes, a comb, a towel, and a few books, he returned it. After that, when Muir passed through cities, he chose to sleep in graveyards, where no bandits would find him.

Muir finally reached the end of his thousand-mile walk at Ceder Key, Florida. Along the way he had become sick with malaria. He stayed in Florida until his health returned, then visited Cuba. Next, he went to New York City and booked passage on a ship to California. Upon arriving in San Francisco, Muir asked the first person he saw, "Which way to the wilderness?" The stranger pointed towards Oakland, and off Muir went. Soon he had walked over 100 miles (160.9 kilometers) to Yosemite, where "the hills are so covered with flowers they seem to be painted."

One of many beautiful views of Yosemite National Park.

The Man of the Mountains

The glorious beauty of the Yosemite Valley and the Sierra Nevada Mountains inspired a cascade of words from Muir. The mountains were "wholly composed of light, like the wall of some celestial city." He called the mountains "The Range of Light." "We are now in the mountains and they are in us," he wrote. They are "making every nerve quiver, filling every pore and cell." When he reached Yosemite Valley, he "shouted and gestured in a wild burst of ecstasy."

Canyons were "mountain streets full of life and light." The river sang with "a thousand songful voices." "Yosemite," he wrote, "was an immense hall or temple lighted from above, where Nature had gathered her choicest treasures."

Working only when he had to, Muir spent all his spare time studying Yosemite's flowers, waterfalls, and mountain peaks. He jotted down his observations in his dog-eared notebook. These notes grew into magazine articles. Many people living in the East were fascinated by his writings and Muir's fanciful descriptions of Yosemite changed their attitudes about wild lands. It was popular at the time to think of the wilderness as an enemy to be conquered by humans, but Muir wrote about nature as a kind friend in need of help.

By 1869, the first cross-country railroad began bringing tourists to Yosemite. In the following years, thousands more arrived—many because of Muir's articles. The most famous authors of the day, including Ralph Waldo Emerson, came to California to meet John Muir —the self-described "tramp." Muir charmed them, one and all.

Muir explored the Grand Canyon in Arizona, the Canyonlands of Utah, the dry hills of Nevada, and the Olympic Peninsula in Washington. "The Mountains are calling me and I must go," he wrote. The harder the climb and the stormier the weather, the happier Muir felt.

*John Burroughs (L), an American naturalist,
author and friend of John Muir (R).*

The Dangers of Ice and Snow

John Muir had many close calls with nature's fury. One day, on top of 14,162-foot (4,317-meter) Mount Shasta, Muir and a friend were caught by a sudden storm. The temperature dropped 22 degrees in minutes and soon went below zero. "Hail gave away to snow," Muir later wrote. "The wind boomed and surged amid the desolate crags; lightning flashes cut the gloomy darkness." The snow blocked their path and the men could not find a way down. Without food, blankets, or firewood, they were trapped.

To stay warm, Muir and his friend jumped in a nearby hot spring. The water was so hot, it burned their skin. The two of them spent the night broiling their backsides in the burning mud while the snow and cold froze their topsides. The springs also gave off poisonous gas fumes. Muir and his friend shouted and shook each other to stay awake so they would not surrender to the fumes.

By dawn the men were "frozen, blistered, famished and numb...all dead but the eyes." When the sun came up, they stumbled down the mountain. Muir's frostbitten feet never quite recovered from the ordeal. But even this frightful experience could not dampen his love of the mountains. While recovering, he wrote glowingly of the stars that night. The tortures "vanished like a dream."

At the age of forty, Muir took off to Alaska. Traveling in a canoe paddled by Indian guides, Muir explored a vast wilderness called Glacier Bay. While traveling alone on one of his many trips, Muir became trapped in a blizzard as night was falling. The only way back to camp was across an ice bridge that loomed over a deep canyon. The ice crackled dangerously as Muir crawled 70 feet (21.7 meters) across the ice bridge. The slightest slip on the ice would have sent Muir plunging down a thousand feet onto the rocks of a rushing river. With typical luck and skill, Muir survived the ordeal. "The glacier almost got me this time," he wrote.

A hot spring geyser erupting in Yellowstone National Park.

Father of the National Forests

When he returned to California, Muir married Louie Wanda Strentzel. He moved to his wife's family farm and made a good bit of money growing Bartlett pears and Tokay grapes. Muir and his wife had two daughters. For almost ten years, he gave up his wilderness treks and writing. His time was taken up with dusty rows of fruit trees and farm chores. But his health got worse. His wife decided that he must return to the wilderness to get strong again.

In 1889, Muir finally returned to the mountains only to discover they had changed. Yosemite had been damaged by tourists, ranchers, and loggers. Muir's beloved flowers had disappeared under the feet of thousands of sheep, which he called "hoofed locusts." A friend of his, Robert Underwood Johnson, suggested that Muir campaign to save Yosemite. Yellowstone National Park had been established by Congress twenty years earlier. Perhaps Yosemite could be protected in the same way.

Muir wrote several articles in *Century Magazine* about the wonders of Yosemite. He also told of the dangers the area faced. He described in detail the land's destruction by ranchers and loggers. In 1890, the United States Congress passed a law creating Yosemite National Park.

After this success, Muir lobbied for protection of other delicate lands. Because of his efforts, people today still enjoy Mount Rainier National Park in Washington and the Petrified Forest National Monument in Arizona, among other places.

Saving such huge areas of wilderness might have been enough for some, but Muir was not satisfied. He wrote dozens of letters to President Benjamin Harrison, who acted on Muir's encouragement to set aside 13 million acres (5.26 million hectares) in Wyoming, Colorado, and California for the country's first national forests. Later, President Grover Cleveland set aside another 21 million acres (8.5 million hectares) of national forest.

With the encouragement of John Muir, U.S. President Grover
Cleveland set aside 21 million acres (8.5 million hectares)
of land to be dedicated to national forests.

This led Muir's fans to give him the title "Father of the American National Forest." When politicians and loggers tried to undo Muir's work, he wrote, "Any fool can destroy trees. Trees cannot run away; and if they could, they would still be destroyed—chased and hunted down as long as fun or a dollar could be got out of their bark hides, branching horns, or magnificent bole backbones."

In 1892, a group of concerned men met in San Francisco and formed the Sierra Club to protect the wilderness of America. John Muir became the club's president.

Three years later, Muir published his first full-length book, *The Mountains of California*. In 1901, he published *Our National Parks*. Both books sold well and his wit and wisdom made him a famous man.

Muir traveled to Alaska with millionaire railroad man, Edward H. Harriman. Harriman was so impressed with Muir's conversation that he hired a secretary to follow Muir around and write down everything he said. These notes were later turned into the book, *Story of My Boyhood and Youth*.

Later in life, John Muir traveled to Europe and South America. In the United States he was as famous as any writer of the day, including Mark Twain. John Muir continued to fight for the wilderness until he was 76 years old. Then, on the day before Christmas, December 24, 1914, he died.

Though John Muir is gone, his spirit still lives in dozens of places that he helped preserve for all people. His memory survives in the Sierra Club, one of the oldest and most famous environmental organizations in history. Today, anyone can benefit from Muir's advice:

Keep close to Nature's heart, yourself;
and break clear away, once in a while, and
climb a mountain or spend a week in the
woods. Wash your spirit clean...

John Muir and his dog in a northern California forest.

RACHEL CARSON
A Delicate Web of Life Destroyed

The wetland marsh was coming alive in the pre-dawn light. As the sun rose over the surrounding pines, thousands of creatures began their daily routines. Delicate trails of vapor slithered over the surface as the warm solar rays hit the water. A chorus of clicking, chirping, tweeting, and whistling grew steadily louder. Animals, birds, and bugs who lived by day awoke to the morning's light. Night creatures nestled into their burrows, under leaves, and in log holes. Marsh plants, bathed in a hundred tones of green, brown, purple, blue, yellow, and red, swayed in the gentle breeze. The air smelled of the nearby salty ocean, the blooming flowers, the mud, and trees. Patterns of life defined by a thousand generations of animals fell neatly into place.

Suddenly, there was a low rumble in the distance—an airplane. The dark machine broke low over the trees and swooped down on the marsh with a roar. As it flew by, it opened sprayer jets on its wings. A cloud of oily, brown liquid rained down. Every living thing below was bathed in a stinking, slippery oil. Again and again, the plane passed over, dumping its payload of DDT in fuel oil on the marsh.

The year was 1957. The plane was spraying the marsh for the government of Plymouth County, Massachusetts. Mosquitos had been a problem that year. Mosquitos lived in marshes and swamps. The insecticide DDT was known to kill mosquitos. Spray the swamps with DDT and kill the mosquitos. It was that simple. Or was it?

Within weeks much of the marsh was dying. The mosquitos were gone, but so were many of the song birds, bees, mice, snakes, frogs, crickets and untold thousands of other creatures. All had been killed by a toxic insecticide: DDT.

Rachel Carson (1907-1964), environmentalist and author of Silent Spring.

The War on Pests

In the 1950s, scenes such as this were common throughout the United States and the rest of the world. To understand why, we must look at history. After World War II ended in 1945, the United States became the world's leading power. New inventions-including plastics, televisions, jet airplanes, computers, and atomic energy-that were developed to fight the war were put to peace-time use.

Some of the by-products of this technological revolution were herbicides, insecticides, and fungicides — commonly called pesticides. The suffix "-cide" is Latin for "killer," so insect-i-cide means "insect killer," and pest-i-cide, "pest killer."

During World War II, the United States developed dozens of poisons to kill humans on the battlefield. Scientists noticed that some of these chemicals also killed insects and plants. After the war, the companies that manufactured these chemicals had nowhere to sell them. They decided to put them to work killing the two biggest enemies of the farmer: bugs and weeds. At that time, there were many people living with hunger and starvation all over the world. People thought these "miracle" chemicals would allow more food production and that insecticides could kill bugs that spread diseases such as malaria and typhus. Some people saw a future where all insect pests would be wiped out.

Starting in the early 1950s, much of the world went on a pesticide binge. Wherever a bug or weed caused a nuisance it was sprayed with a chemical poison. Fruit growers fogged trees with pesticides to kill caterpillars. Electric companies sprayed herbicides along power lines to kill trees and weeds. Cities sprayed lakes and marshes to kill mosquitos. In some places, people who had fleas or lice were hosed down with DDT.

Many gardeners sprayed poisons all over their vegetable gardens. The companies that made these chemicals advertised them as modern miracles with no side effects. People believed that they could control nature and get rid of any plant or animal that bothered them.

24

Crop-dusting machine spraying insecticide over a broccoli field.

Silent Killer

By 1960, production of pesticides in the United States had increased more than five fold, from 125 million pounds (56.6 million kilograms) in 1947 to 666 million pounds (301.6 million kilograms) in 1960. That was equal to almost four pounds (1.8 kilograms) of pesticides for every man, woman, and child in the country. The companies that manufactured these chemicals made billions of dollars in profit.

DDT (short for dichloro-diphenyl-trichloro-ethane), the most popular poison of the time, was invented by a German chemist in 1874. But the chemical was not used as a pesticide until 1939, when it was hailed as a way to stamp out insect pests and help farmers grow more food. The man who discovered this use for DDT, Swiss chemist Paul Müller, won a Nobel Prize for his work. The chemical's first use was dusting thousands of soldiers, refugees, and prisoners of war in World War II to kill lice.

By the late 1950s, some people noticed that something was out of kilter. For one thing, the bugs that pesticides were supposed to kill were no longer affected by the chemicals. In fact, after a spraying there seemed to be more bugs than before. Farmers noticed that each year they had to increase the amount of pesticides they sprayed on their fields. By 1960, there were 137 species of bugs pesticides would not kill. Today there are over 400.

There were other, less obvious problems. Certain kinds of birds and "good" insects were slowly disappearing. Chemicals that were only supposed to be found on dead bugs were turning up in drinking water and in human beings. DDT would not break down; it remained in the soil and water for years. No amount of sun, rain, water, or bacteria would eliminate it. If it were sprayed on a bug, it went into the bird that ate the bug, into the cat that ate the bird, and so on.

Pesticides sprayed on fruits and vegetables entered the humans who ate them. But this was known to only a few scientists—that is, until Rachel Carson told them.

Images of the Ocean

Rachel Louise Carson was born in Springdale, Pennsylvania, on May 27, 1907. She was the youngest of three children, and a delicate girl. Often her health was bad. Many days, while her brother and sister were in school, Rachel's mother, Maria, would keep her at home and the two of them would go for long walks on the family farm. Maria had been a school teacher and she took delight in telling Rachel the names of the plants, bugs, birds, and animals who lived on their farm. Carson wrote stories and painted pictures of the local wildlife. She enjoyed the farm life and living close to nature.

Carson's farm was an island of beauty in the middle of Pennsylvania's industrial heartland. The hills surrounding the farm had been stripmined for coal, leaving them dead and lifeless. Nearby factories blackened the sky with pollution. The river ran yellow with industrial chemicals. Because of this, Carson was exposed to the dangers of chemical pollution at an early age.

When Carson was ten years old, World War I started. Her brother, Robert, joined the Army air force and wrote her letters about bombings, air battles, and heroic soldiers. Fascinated, Carson wrote a story called "A Battle In the Clouds," and sent it to a children's magazine. The magazine printed the story and mailed Carson a check for ten dollars. Then and there, Carson decided that she wanted to be an author.

In the 1920s, most women did not attend college, but Carson was an exceptional student. After high school she earned a scholarship to the Pennsylvania College for Women (later renamed Chatham College). There she majored in English literature and published stories in the school magazine. One of her stories, "The Master of the Ship's Light," contained vivid images of towering waves and other powerful visions of the sea. But Carson had never seen the ocean.

Rachel Carson

Rachel Carson studied biology in college and majored in zoology.

Amazing Fish Tales

Carson studied biology in college and it soon became her favorite subject. She decided to major in marine zoology—the study of animal life in the ocean. Meshing her love of the ocean with her writing skills and zoology degree, Carson graduated from college in 1929 with high honors.

In the 1920s, science was considered a "men only" profession. But Carson's high marks gained her a full scholarship to Johns Hopkins University in Baltimore where she obtained a master's degree in zoology.

The summer before she was to enter graduate school, Carson finally swam in the ocean for the first time. She won an internship at Woods Hole Marine Biological Laboratory on Cape Cod in Massachusetts. Now the woman who had written so beautifully about the ocean and studied it so carefully could actually feel its foamy waves.

After she graduated from college, Carson had a difficult time finding work in her field. There was an economic depression sweeping the country and millions of people were without jobs. The fact that she was a woman working in a "man's field" lessened her job prospects. For a while Carson taught at the University of Maryland. She also continued to write, publishing articles about marine life in the *Baltimore Sunday Sun*.

In 1935, Carson's father died suddenly and she needed extra money to support her mother. As luck would have it, she landed a job writing scripts for a radio show about marine life. The show was called "Romance Under the Waters" and was sponsored by the Bureau of Fisheries, part of the U. S. Fish and Wildlife Service. In the studio, however, the show was jokingly called "Amazing Fish Tales." Soon Carson was appointed junior aquatic biologist by the bureau. Her work for the Fish and Wildlife Service became a career. In 1949, she became chief of all publications by the bureau.

Carson continued writing, and in 1941 she published her first book, *Under the Sea Wind.* The book explains the almost magical workings of the ocean. Reviewers praised Carson for presenting scientific fact in an easy-to-read story.

But the book was released just weeks before the United States entered World War II. People had their minds on other matters and the book sold very poorly.

Carson continued to work for the government during the war years. When she had spare time, she traveled to the Florida Everglades or to a cabin in Maine to study wildlife. She even explored underwater, wearing a diving helmet and lead boots.

Best Seller

In 1950, Carson released her second book, *The Sea Around Us.* This book was a detailed study of the sea. It explained depths, currents, animal life, and underwater land forms. *The Sea Around Us* became an instant hit, spending 81 weeks on the New York Times bestseller list. *Under the Sea Wind* was released again, and it became a bestseller, too.

With the money from her publishing success, Carson quit her job at the Fisheries Bureau. She built a cottage among the pine trees and granite rocks of the Maine seacoast. There she dedicated all her time to writing, and published *The Edge of the Sea* in 1955. Carson also wrote a book about her walks with her grandnephew, called *A Sense of Wonder.*

Silent Spring

Rachel Carson had become an expert on the ocean's ecology and an American celebrity. During her years as a government employee she had done research on the effects of DDT on wildlife. She had tried to write articles about the danger of the chemical but could find no interested publishers. One day a friend wrote her a letter about the spraying of DDT on a nearby marsh. The friend described dead song-birds in her garden and robins falling out of trees. Carson decided to take action about DDT and began research for her next book, *Silent Spring.*

In this book, Carson explained the dangers of pesticides in vivid detail. She cited study after study showing the dangers of DDT. She explained in simple terms the chemistry of the poisons and how they affect all life. Her book sounded a warning that all life on Earth was endangered if human beings kept poisoning the planet. She warned that future generations would look back and wonder how people could have been so careless.

Carson's words best tell the story: "For the first time in the history of the world, every human being is now subjected to contact with dangerous chemicals. They occur virtually everywhere. They have been recovered from most of the major river systems and even from streams of groundwater flowing unseen through the earth. They have been found in fish in remote mountain lakes, in earthworms burrowing in soil, in the eggs of birds—and in man himself."

While writing the book about cancer-causing chemicals, Rachel Carson herself got cancer. A tumor was removed from her breast. She continued writing but, tragically, the cancer continued to spread through her body.

DDT

Japanese beetles after being sprayed with DDT.

When *Silent Spring* was published it hit like a bombshell. The chemical industry called Rachel Carson a crank and a kook. They claimed that a woman could not understand their complicated chemicals. Farmers' groups were against the book. They feared returning to the days of crop failures and insect plagues. The American Medical Association debated her figures about cancer, saying the chemicals had not been around long enough for people to be sure of their affects.

At the same time, millions of angry citizens called the government. They demanded to know why they weren't warned of the dangers of pesticides. President John F. Kennedy ordered the Office of Science and Technology to study the book. These scientists agreed with Carson's findings. Carson herself testified on television before a Senate committee formed to study the problem. Her book brought her many honors and many enemies.

On April 14, 1964, Rachel Carson died of cancer. While she was no longer able to fight against chemical pollution, her book had a worldwide impact. It was reprinted in fourteen languages. DDT was banned from sale in the United States and in many other countries.

Although it is hard to believe, 50 million pounds (22.6 million kilograms) of DDT is still manufactured in the United States every year and sold for use on crops in other countries, including Mexico. Countries in South and Central America still use DDT and many other poisons to kill pests. Food sprayed with DDT is still imported into the United States and sold at many grocery stores. The United States Department of Agriculture still promotes the use of other pesticides for farmers. Safe limits for most of these chemicals have yet to be decided.

Because of Rachel Carson's efforts, the world was awakened to the facts of pesticide use. She fought bravely alone, sometimes fighting the pain of cancer, to sound the alarm for future generations. As a scientist, writer, and environmentalist Rachel Carson will long be remembered as a friend of the Earth. It is up to us to continue her battle against the chemical war on nature.

JACQUES-YVES COUSTEAU
Invisible Life Under the Sea

Though humans have lived upon the Earth for hundreds of thousands of years, they have explored very little of it. It's true that almost every nook and cranny of the land has been trod upon by human feet. But 75 percent of the Earth's surface is covered with water. People's ventures into the sea have been short and often dangerous. Many have managed to skim the surface of the oceans in boats, sailing here and there with some success. But until recently the region beneath the waves, where all life on Earth began, remained a mystery to all. That's because no one can live without air for more than a few minutes. Unable to breathe underwater, human beings had no idea who or what lived in the ocean for many centuries.

Today all that has changed. People can simply turn on their televisions and learn about the enchanting realm of underwater worlds. Modern breathing equipment and waterproof cameras have opened up a new universe filled with strange and breath-taking beauty. Some underwater creatures look like they swam out of a science-fiction movie. Coral caves, grottos, hot bubbling lava, and other underwater formations have the unworldly look of other planets.

Modern inventions help us enjoy underwater life, but they also show us humanity's effects on the ocean: coral dead from water pollution, underwater animal species facing extinction, plastic garbage and fishing nets in the most remote places. In the short time since humans have been able to explore the oceans, we have also begun to save them.

In the world of undersea exploration and education, one person stands above the rest as a world-class researcher and environmentalist: Jacques-Yves Cousteau.

Marine explorer, Captain Jacques-Yves Cousteau.

Like a Fish to Water

Jacques-Yves Cousteau (pronounced "koo-STOW") was born on June 11, 1910, in a small village near the French port city of Bordeaux. His father was a lawyer who worked for several American millionaires. Because of his father's work, Jacques and his family traveled constantly. Cousteau's first memory is falling asleep to the rocking rhythm of a train. During the summer the family stayed in their seaside home in Royan, France. There, where he spent most of his time splashing in the cold ocean waves, Cousteau developed a life-long fascination with water.

In 1920, the Cousteau family moved to New York for a year and "Jack," as he was called by his American friends, learned to speak English. At summer camp in Vermont, his counselors remember him diving deep into the lake, sometimes twelve feet down. Cousteau was selected to clear branches from the bottom of the lake under the diving board because of his diving skills. He took to the job like a fish to water.

Cousteau's family lived in Paris when they returned to France. Young Jacques was not a good student and preferred tinkering with inventions and writing. When he was twelve, he built a giant model of a machine used to unload cargo from ships. Cousteau also wrote his first story, *The Adventure in Mexico*. He lettered and illustrated the book by hand and ran off copies on a mimeograph machine.

Ignoring his schoolwork, Cousteau bought a used movie camera and began his own one-boy movie company called FILMS ZIX. Cousteau was the producer, director, and cameraman. He loved to develop his own film and tinker with the camera. Seeing the camera as a distraction, his father took it away for a while. Cousteau's grades improved.

After a window-breaking spree at school, Cousteau was expelled in disgrace. He was sent to a boarding school in the Alsace region of France where discipline was strictly enforced. Under the watchful eye of his teachers, Cousteau became a very good student. When he graduated, he easily past the test for entrance into the French Naval Academy. Jacques-Yves Cousteau was ready to see the world.

Tragedy Strikes

With his movie camera under his arm, Cousteau boarded a ship full of other naval trainees and set sail for a one-year cruise around the world. Cousteau studied, filmed, and wrote in his spare moments aboard the training ship. He graduated second in his class in 1933, and at the age of twenty-three became a French naval officer. Next, the ambitious Cousteau enrolled in flying school to become a fighter pilot. But one night, on a darkened road, his life was changed forever.

Cousteau had borrowed his father's sports car to drive to a friend's wedding. He was speeding along a desolate mountain road when the car's lights went out. Cousteau slammed on the brakes but the car flew off the road into a dark abyss. When he awoke, he was in severe pain. He had broken several ribs, one of his arms was shattered, and the other arm was paralyzed. Cousteau pulled himself from the wreckage and crawled, broken and bleeding, to a nearby farmhouse. He knocked on the door at two a.m. At first the woman inside yelled, "Go away!" But after she saw Cousteau's condition she called a doctor.

Cousteau was rushed to a hospital and bandaged up. His right arm was so badly damaged that doctors wanted to amputate it. Cousteau refused to allow this. They said he would never use either of his arms again. Still, he refused to let the doctors cut off his arm.

Cousteau was determined to heal himself. He spent long hours soaking in whirlpool baths. He tried exercise and other cures. After eight months, he was able to move one finger. At ten months, he could move two fingers and one wrist. Cousteau doggedly pursued his exercises until he regained the use of his arms, although one arm remained slightly twisted.

Underwater Jungle

After his recovery, the navy stationed Cousteau in Toulon, France, on the Mediterranean Sea. He kept up his healing exercise, swimming hour after hour to strengthen his arms. Another sailor showed Cousteau a pair of underwater goggles used by Japanese pearl divers. The minute he dived beneath the water wearing the goggles, his life was set on a new course.

"I saw fish," Cousteau later recalled. "Standing up to breathe, I saw a trolley car, people, electric light poles. I put my eyes under again, and civilization just vanished. I was in a jungle never before seen by those who floated on top of the opaque sea."

Cousteau wanted to dive deeper and deeper as soon as he saw the wondrous world beneath the waves. He fashioned an air tube from a garden hose so he could stay under longer. When he wasn't diving he worked to solve the problems faced by undersea divers.

In 1937, Cousteau married Simone Melchior, whose father was an admiral in the navy and came from a long line of French admirals. The couple had two sons, Phillipe and Jean-Michel.

When World War II broke out in Europe in 1939, Nazi Germany quickly conquered France, and soon the French navy was disarmed. Cousteau lived in the hills above Toulon to pursue his interest in diving. He tried breathing pure oxygen out of a tank, but found this made him giddy. He tried coating his body with thick grease to protect him from the cold water. This, too, was a failure.

*Scientist, explorer and motion picture producer
Capt. Jacques-Yves Cousteau, shown here demonstrating
his invention, the aqua-lung (1950).*

Scuba Breakthrough

Cousteau decided that compressed air in a tank was the solution to the problem of being able to breathe underwater. The tank needed a special valve that would open when the diver inhaled and close when he or she exhaled. Cousteau visited Air Liquide, a company that made compressed air tanks in Paris, where his wife's father worked. He met a scientist there, Émile Gagnan, who happened to be working on a valve to allow cars to run on natural gas. The valve was just what Cousteau needed.

In June 1943, after a few changes on the valve, Cousteau tried his new invention, which he called the Self-Contained Underwater Breathing Apparatus, or SCUBA. Cousteau strapped on the 50-pound (22.6-kilogram) air tanks, put on flippers and a face mask, and made the world's first scuba dive. Cousteau swam underwater loops, did somersaults, and stood upside down, balancing on one finger. He swam into a cave full of lobsters, plucked one up and gave it to Simone, who was swimming above. The scuba was a success and the lobster made for a delicious dinner.

Cousteau wanted to make movies underwater so that everyone could enjoy the beauty he had discovered there. But there was a film shortage in France because of the war. The Nazis would not permit Cousteau to buy movie film. To get around this problem, Cousteau and Simone traveled from town to town buying short rolls of film used in still cameras. The film had to be handled in total darkness, so Cousteau sat under a blanket and taped the short rolls of film together to make one long roll for his movie camera. Cousteau fashioned a waterproof case for his camera, carefully loaded the film, and took the world's first undersea movies. Later, two short films of his friends exploring a sunken wreck and feeding fish won prizes at the Cannes Film Festival.

While Cousteau spent much of his time perfecting his inventions, he had other work to do. As a member of the French underground resistance he spied on the German army. German soldiers who were watching Cousteau thought he was simply diving and fishing. But he was secretly recording German ships entering and leaving the port. On one mission, Cousteau slipped into enemy headquarters dressed as an Italian soldier. (The Italians fought on the German side in WW II.) Cousteau photographed code books and other top-secret papers with a tiny camera. After the war, France rewarded him with its highest medals, the Legion of Honor and the War Cross.

Submarine base

Jacques Cousteau is an inventor, among other things. Here he is explaining his concept and design for a five-man underwater submarine base (1964).

Captain of the Calypso

When the war ended, Cousteau formed the Undersea Research Group. They performed dangerous work, such as finding and disarming live underwater mines that had been left behind by the Nazis. On one dive the group found a two-thousand-year-old Roman shipwreck.

Cousteau's films and inventions made him a worldwide celebrity. Magazine editors, television producers, and filmmakers were clamoring for his underwater photography skills. Industries and developers were hungry for his ideas about undersea pipelines, ocean-floor mining, and ship design.

One result of Cousteau's success was a huge increase in scuba diving. By the mid-1950s, millions of people all over the world had strapped on scuba gear and tried underwater exploration themselves.

But Cousteau's interests lay in scientific research. What he needed was a ship. In 1950, Cousteau bought an old mine sweeper from the United States and named it the *Calypso* after a Greek water nymph. The ship was full of complicated oceanography equipment, formerly used by the United States Navy. Because it was made for finding submerged mines, the ship had an underwater chamber made of glass. There, a person could lie on their stomach and stare down into the depths of the sea.

The Cousteau family and a sizable crew traveled everywhere on the Calypso: the Atlantic Ocean, the Pacific Ocean, the Red Sea, the Indian Ocean, Alaska, Antarctica, and even the Amazon River. With a spirit of fun and a sense of adventure, the crew explored sunken ships, coral, underwater caves, fishes, and ocean life. All the while they filmed movies and shot photographs.

In 1953, Cousteau wrote his first book, *The Silent World,* which became a bestseller. Four years later, a movie based on the book won an Academy Award for Cousteau.

Jacques-Yves Cousteau's famed research vessel, the Calypso, *arrives in St. Louis for a documentary on the Mississippi River (1985).*

French explorer Jacques-Yves Cousteau poses in front of the model of a revolutionary ship which will be called the Calypso II *(1992). The* Calypso II *will be connected to satellites to gather and deliver environmental data from anywhere in the world.*

Not content with the limitations of scuba gear, Cousteau wanted to go deeper than the equipment would allow. So he invented a two-person diving saucer, a one-person mini-submarine, and a "house under the sea" where people could stay underwater for weeks at a time. With every new invention, new scientific discoveries about the ocean quickly followed.

As exciting as it was, life aboard the *Calypso* was more than fun and games. Diving in deep water is dangerous. There was often fear of sharks attacking divers and Cousteau and his divers had many close calls with sharks. "Rapture of the deep," another danger facing underwater explorers, causes divers to see visions and sometimes lose their minds due to heavy water pressure. Some divers pull their face masks off thinking that they can breathe water. One of the divers aboard the *Calypso* died when he did this at a depth of 400 feet (122 meters). Other divers with rapture want to stay underwater forever and refuse to come up. Divers sometimes rise too quickly to the surface and get the "bends," a crippling illness. Despite these dangers, Cousteau continued his research.

Underwater explorer Jacques Cousteau (L) and former U.S. Senator Al Gore chat during a break in a conference on environmental issues during the Earth Summit in Rio De Janeiro (1992).

Pollution in the Fragile Sea

By the 1960s, Cousteau's film specials were regular events on television. Millions of people were shown how beautiful—and fragile—the oceans were. In his travels, Cousteau noticed the oceans were changing. He found garbage and pollution in the most remote parts of the ocean, thousands of miles from land. He testified about the damages of pollution at congressional hearings in Washington, D. C.

"People do not realize that all pollution ends up in the sea," Cousteau said in early 1970s. "It is washed by the rain which carries everything into the oceans, where life has diminished forty percent in the past twenty years." When people heard this, they were shocked that almost half of all ocean life had been effected in only twenty years.

In 1973, Cousteau set up the Cousteau Society in Norfolk, Virginia, to protect and preserve the oceans. Today it has over 300,000 members. He continues to educate people about the oceans with his books and films. To date, Cousteau has written 50 books and made more than 60 television documentaries about his life and the sea.

Jacques Cousteau's inventive mind and quest for knowledge changed the way the world sees and thinks about the oceans. He has shown us incredible mysteries of the deep. He has proven that it is our responsibility to save the oceans. The Cousteau Society continues to lobby the United Nations for strict worldwide laws against pollution.

Scientists believe that all life once came from the sea. Thanks to Jacques-Yves Cousteau, humanity may yet save our ancient home.

Glossary

Aquatic - Living or growing in the water.

Avalanche - A large mass of snow rapidly sliding down a mountain.

Botany - The study of plant life.

DDT - An insecticide; short for dichloro-diphenyl-trichloro-ethane.

Desertification - When formerly fertile land becomes barren and dry like a desert.

Ecology - The study of how plants and animals relate to the world around them.

Extinct - Animals (and plants) that no longer exist.

Fungicide - Chemicals used for destroying fungi such as mold.

Grotto - A cave or cavern.

Groundwater - Fresh water that gathers in pools beneath the surface of the ground.

Herbicide - Chemicals used for killing plants such as weeds.

Insecticide - Chemicals used for killing insects.

Lice - Small wingless insects that live on human beings and other animals.

Lobby - To try to influence the vote of a lawmaking body.

Marine zoology - The science of studying animals that live in the sea.

Naturalist - A person who studies natural history, including botany, zoology, and ecology.

Oceanography - The science that deals with the ocean.

Pesticide - Any chemical that kills pests such as insects, fungus, or plants.

Preserved - To keep safe from harm.

Scuba - A portable breathing devise used for underwater exploration.

Sequoia trees - Evergreen trees that are the tallest trees on Earth.

Strip-mine - An open-pit mine made by stripping off the top layer of dirt.

Zoology - The study of animal life.

Index

Target Earth™ Commitment

At Target, we're committed to the environment. We show this commitment not only through our own internal efforts but also through the programs we sponsor in the communities where we do business.

Our commitment to children and the environment began when we became the Founding International Sponsor for Kids for Saving Earth, a non-profit environmental organization for kids. We helped launch the program in 1989 and supported its growth to three-quarters of a million club members in just three years.

Our commitment to children's environmental education led to the development of an environmental curriculum called Target Earth™, aimed at getting kids involved in their education and in their world.

In addition, we worked with Abdo & Daughters Publishing to develop the Target Earth™ Earthmobile, an environmental science library on wheels that can be used in libraries, or rolled from classroom to classroom.

Target believes that the children are our future and the future of our planet. Through education, they will save the world!

TARGET.

Minneapolis-based Target Stores is an upscale discount department store chain of 517 stores in 33 states coast-to-coast, and is the largest division of Dayton Hudson Corporation, one of the nation's leading retailers.